Heart of Compassion

Other books
by Gerald Vann
available from
Sophia Institute Press:

At the Foot of the Cross
The Devil: And How to Resist Him
The Seven Sweet Blessings of Christ

Gerald Vann, O.P.

Heart of
Compassion

The Vocation of Woman Today

SOPHIA INSTITUTE PRESS®
Manchester, New Hampshire

Heart of Compassion: The Vocation of Woman Today was originally published in London in 1946 by Blackfriars Publications under the title *Eve and the Gryphon*. This 1998 edition by Sophia Institute Press, published with the kind permission of the English Province of the Order of Preachers, includes slight editorial revisions throughout the text.

Printed in the United States of America
Jacket design by Lorraine Bilodeau

The cover artwork is a detail of Eustache
Leseur's *Christ Carrying the Cross*, The Louvre,
Paris, France (Art Resource, New York).

Sophia Institute Press®
Box 5284, Manchester, NH 03108
1-800-888-9344

Nihil Obstat: Thomas E. Bird, D.D., Ph.D.
Imprimatur: Humphrey Bright, *Vicarius Capitularis*
Birmingham, June 5, 1946

Library of Congress Cataloging-in-Publication Data

Vann, Gerald, 1906-1963.
    [Eve and the gryphon]
    Heart of compassion : the vocation of woman today / Gerald
      Vann.
    p. cm.
    Originally published : Eve and the gryphon. Oxford : Blackfriars
      Publications, 1946.
    ISBN 0-918477-76-X (pbk. : alk. paper)
    1. Catholic women — Religious life. I. Title.
BX2353.V34 1998
282'.082 — dc21   98-20415 CIP

98 99 00 01 02   10 9 8 7 6 5 4 3 2 1

Contents

Editor's Note: The biblical references in the following pages are based on the Douay-Rheims edition of the Old and New Testaments. Where applicable, quotations have been cross-referenced with the differing names and enumeration in the Revised Standard Version, using the following symbol: (RSV =).

Preface

✤

The following pages seem to call for an initial word of apology. My excuse for writing on a subject about which I must necessarily be supposed to know nothing is, first of all, that having ventured to give some conferences to St. Joan's Alliance at Oxford on the vocation of woman, I was urged to put down what I had said in writing; and secondly, that my main concern is not with the facts of married life but with the theology that lies behind them, and I do not know that mistakes about the facts need invalidate the attempt to state the theological principles.

I must emphasize also that what follows will necessarily be a one-sided picture of life precisely because it is concerned with the vocation of woman and not of man. A great many of the things which are here said to apply to women would also apply, although no doubt from a different angle, to men. As it is, I have been concerned to describe what, as it seems to me, women ought to be trying to do. In other words, I have attempted to describe the ideal; whereas, insofar as man comes into the picture, he comes in less as he ought to be than as he usually is — not the ideal but the real. It is necessary to stress this fact, lest it appear that one is unfairly discriminating, and putting all the influences for good on one side of the total picture to the exclusion of the other. The man has his equally great and equally essential part to play, but to describe that could not come within the plan of this book.

To say that one is describing the ideal also calls for a word of caution. You need to know the ideal, so as to be quite clear what you are aiming at; but that does not alter the fact that in real life you never attain it, and are often tempted to despair of ever even remotely approaching it. In this context, moreover, you may be tempted to despair not only of yourself but of the other, or others, with whom your life has to be shared; to do your part successfully is not a thing that depends on you alone. It should, then, be borne in mind throughout the following pages that, if the picture they paint of the ideal is the true one, the fact that reality seems little likely to approximate to it in any measurable future is no cause for discouragement. This Rome, like many others and more than most, will not be built in a day; and often you may find that while the surface of things looks black indeed, there are hidden processes, going on beneath the surface, which are full of promise. And in any case you will find eventually that, in the most important sense, to have tried is to have achieved. You do the best you can, and leave it to God to decide what the measure of success shall be; you sow, but the reaping you leave to His wisdom and His love.

Gerald Vann

✤

Heart of Compassion

❧

Strive for union with God

Seek ye first the kingdom of Heaven.
Matthew 6:33

※

"Seek ye first," said our Lord, "the kingdom of Heaven."[1] We are to think, in these meditations, of the vocation of Catholic women living in the world and trying to work for Christ in the world; and I want to consider with you some of the great basic facts by which, as it seems to me, any such life must be guided and shaped. In order to do that, I want to set before you the figures of four great Catholic women, or rather of three great Catholic women and one great symbol of Catholic womanhood. And first let us think of St. Catherine of Siena (c. 1333-1380).

We have been told by the Vicar of Christ[2] that this is to be an age of Catholic action, an age in which the

---

[1] Matt. 6:33.
[2] Pope Pius XII (1876-1958).

Church's life is to be especially expressed, and Her redeeming work in the world especially fulfilled, by the lay people; and St. Catherine might well be the patron of woman's share in that apostolate. She was a religious, it is true — she is the great glory of the Third Order of St. Dominic — but she lived and worked in the world as any Dominican tertiary may do today; and she used her immense wisdom and power to do just the sort of work that most needs doing today. You have to follow where she led.

She was, I suppose, the greatest woman of her century; she was certainly one of the greatest women Europe has ever seen. She began with no advantages of birth, education, or influence; yet we find her overcoming all opposition, acquiring an international renown, advising princes, and being called upon to arbitrate between contending states: inducing the Pope, in the teeth of powerful opposition, to return to Rome from Avignon, being herself called to Rome later on to help in the shaping of papal policy, and playing a part of unique importance when the terrible scandal of the great schism fell upon the Church. Where did her power come from? What had gone before?

There are two lessons we must learn from her.

�֍

Holiness and wisdom are grounded in love

We are told that once when her confessor was preaching in the Dominican church, word was brought to him that Catherine was dead. He refused to believe it, finished his sermon, and then went to her house, where he found her apparently lifeless and surrounded by weeping friends and disciples. Still he refused to believe that she was dead and took her hand, and presently she did indeed return to consciousness of her surroundings. And then she in her turn could only weep, and repeat over and over again, "Oh, I am so unhappy." She explained later on, "I have seen the secret things of God." And she could not bear to come back from them to the world of sin and suffering and blindness. But that is not the end of the story. We are told that later on, when Catherine was one day rapt in ecstasy and was begging to be taken back to those secret things that she had seen and possessed for a time, our Lord rebuked her for her *egoism*.

Pope Pius XII, in his encyclical *Mystici Corporis*, applies to the Church the words of St. Paul: "The head cannot say to the feet, 'I have no need of you.'"[3] Christ, He

---

[3] Cf. 1 Cor. 12:21.

tells us, *needs* His members, so that His redemptive work in the world may be carried out — not because He is weak, but because He so willed it for the greater glory of the Church. So it is certain that the salvation of many depends on the prayers and penances of Christ's faithful and on the part they play in sharing in His work.

That is the first lesson we must learn from Catherine's story: that there is such a thing as the danger of a selfish pursuit of holiness. If you are trying hard to live the Catholic life, if you are trying daily to find God and to live always close to Him, if you really want, not in sentiment, but in deed and in truth, to put on Christ[4] and be transformed into His likeness, then you have to make sure that you are not forgetting what He said to His Apostles: "By this shall men know you are my disciples, that you have love one for another."[5] You have to make sure that you are not forgetting the words of St. John in his turn: "If any man say, 'I love God,' and hate his brother, he is a liar."[6]

[4]Rom. 13:14; Gal. 3:27.
[5]John 13:35.
[6]1 John 4:20.

For this is indeed the very stuff of Christian holiness. He took upon Himself our humanity that He might raise us to His divinity. You are to put on Christ and so, with Christ and in Christ, to come to union with the Godhead. But this is the God who so loved the world that He sent His only-begotten Son to save it;[7] this is the Christ who saved and saves. And insofar as you do come to this union, which even in this life is your destiny, you cannot remain absorbed in it and forget the world as long as there are souls to save and work to be done in the world. You must come down again from the mountain of vision, still with Christ and in Christ; and in the power of the vision and with all urgency of the love of Christ, you must set yourself to the work He needs you to do.

Wisdom is an end in itself: to try to justify it by its practical effects in terms of power is to degrade it; but at the same time it is perfected, like all experience, when it is expressed and its richness diffused. The Christian ideal of wisdom is not a cold, still, impassable contemplation of abstract truth: it is the vision of the Truth who is also Love, and therefore it necessarily impels us

[7] John 3:16.

to loving activity. That is why we read, in the praise of wisdom in the Old Testament, the assertion, perhaps surprising at first sight, that "wisdom is more active than all active things."[8]

St. Catherine of Siena wrote the book the *Dialogue*, and you would have to search far to find a book written by another that enshrined a deeper wisdom. But it was the same Catherine who toiled in the hospitals of Siena and tended the leper, and who, although in great pain, went to and fro across Europe to bring peace to men. To be truly wise is to have learned to see God, but to see God is also to see and love and labor for the world He has made.

⌘

Love of God must supersede love of others
But there is a second, and complementary, lesson to be learned in this story of Catherine of Siena. Where did she find the power to do the work she did? (For it is not only the immensity of her labors that is so astonishing: it is still more the way in which unlikely people listened to her, were charmed and changed by her, and

[8] Wisd. 7:24.

surrendered to her and obeyed her.) What is it that you must do in your turn if you are to be like her?

The answer is simple. She was reproached for her egoism, but she was already saintly when she was reproached, and her egoism, if you compare it with our mean and niggling little selfishness, was a white-hot fire of selfless love: she had already given herself wholly to God. And that is the hard thing; but it is the essential.

The second danger we have to beware of is the danger of supposing that as long as we love the world and labor for it, as it seems best to us, we have nothing else to do. This is a greater danger than the first. It is wrong to seek God in such a way as to forget our duty to the world, but at least if we do, we are not putting secondary things first. If we think we can help humanity without first trying to find God, if we try to love humanity without trying first of all to love God, then we are indeed subordinating the infinite to the finite; we are in danger of falling into practical idolatry.

And we are in danger also of defeating our own ends, for we like to think that we are quite capable of deciding for ourselves how best to help others, and it is only perhaps when our schemes are brought to nothing and disaster comes upon us that we realize that we are fools.

And then perhaps God leads us, through our better knowledge of ourselves, to a deeper wisdom, and we begin all over again — begin to learn that if we want to love the world in such a way as to help and not harm it, we must first of all listen to God; and that unless we search for Him above all other things, we miss the deepest reality and the primary purpose of life.

We must learn to love with the heart of Christ

To study the life of Catherine, as indeed of any saint, is to realize that true wisdom and power are the fruits of a long, hard struggle: the struggle to find God in the silence and solitude of daily prayer; the struggle to be transformed into His likeness by becoming wholly obedient to His will and so learning the lesson of what is called detachment. As our Lord spent thirty years of hidden preparation for His work, and three years in achieving it, so Catherine in her turn had first her period of solitude and penance, and only then her brilliant spell of work in the world.

Certainly we shall misunderstand her entirely if we think of her during this early period as a dour, thin-lipped, lackluster thing. She was so merry as a child that they nicknamed her Joy. She exulted in the splendors of art which surrounded her, and still her feast is celebrated with flowers because she loved them so much.

But it remains true that for three years she lived in silence, scarcely left the house except to go to church, and subjected herself to an intense asceticism. It was the necessary training for what was to come; it was also the single-minded carrying out of our Lord's injunction, "Seek first the kingdom of Heaven." It was the achieving of the *unum necessarium*, the one thing necessary.[9]

But what was the perfect fruit of this period of trial and training? It was not the vision of the secret things of God during her mystical death, although that in itself is something beyond our aspiring. It was not in her cry to be dissolved and be again with Christ, although that is something of which our earthbound spirits can only dream from afar.

There are four stages in this extraordinary and dramatic life. To see them in their order is to have the two lessons we have been considering combined into one, and it is the third step in the story that is the climax and the clue to the whole.

[9] Cf. Luke 10:42.

Heart of Compassion

It is an incident heavily veiled in mystery. One thing is beyond dispute: however we interpret the thing itself, its meaning for our own lives is clear. The period of intense solitude is over, the secret things have been revealed, and the cry of desire to be united again and forever with Christ has been met with the reproach of egoism. Our Lord is teaching her the lesson of divine love for men. And one day the lesson, we are to suppose, is learned in its fullness. Catherine is in ecstasy, and later she tells her confessor that Christ has appeared to her and taken away her heart. The good man's logical mind is outraged: "If you were without a heart," he tells her, "you would be dead." But she insists that she is telling the truth. And so she goes on for some days, and then our Lord appears to her again and gives her back, not her own heart, but His own.

What does it mean, to have the heart of Christ? It means, in the first place, to be filled entirely with the love of God; but it means also to have within one the love that toiled and suffered and died in compassion and sorrow for the world, and that will not rest until the redemptive process is fulfilled to the end. It is to have the love that will never be quenched by enmity or betrayal, nor disgusted by sin and squalor. It is to have the heart that can draw all things to itself, because it has already given them the power to love by being itself broken on the Cross.

⚓

Union with God should be our goal in all our actions
You have had the stage of preparatory training and searching for God; you have had the stage of complete absorption in the love of God; and now you have this third stage, which is both climax and introduction. It is a climax because here is the completion of growth in union with God, and the entire identity of will with the will of God, which prayer and detachment have wrought. And it is an introduction because the fourth stage inevitably follows as the expression of what has been learned and suffered and done — the stage of unstinted and redemptive sharing in the suffering of the sin-racked world.

And this period, too, has its climax, the further mysterious experience in which Catherine, having now indeed begged to be allowed to take on herself the sin and pain of the Church, felt her shoulders crushed beneath the weight of the *navicella*, the Ship of Peter,[10]

[10]The Ship, or Barque, of Peter, refers to the Church.

and was in fact stricken with a paralysis which ended some days later in her death.

"Seek ye first the kingdom, and the rest shall be added unto you."[11] That is what we learn from the life of Catherine: first we must seek God and be made one with Him, and then we shall turn again to the world — but in true love and wisdom and in the power of God. Only in this way shall we share as we should in the redemptive work of Christ.

It would of course be wrong to suppose that we must wait until we have reached the identity of will with God, which the exchange of hearts symbolizes, before we begin to work in the world. If we did wait, we would achieve little, most of us. But it does mean that we must be clear about the order of importance. It means that we must try, above all, to be united with God in mind and heart and will, lest all the rest be a service, not of the world, but of ourselves. It means that, all the time, we must be schooling ourselves to grow, as Catherine did, in prayer and detachment.

Let us think first of all about the life of prayer. What does it mean? It means three things.

[11]Matt. 6:33.

❧

We must commit ourselves to daily prayer

You may not be called to retire into solitude for a long period as Catherine was; that is not the essential thing. There are plenty of men and women who have learned to be saints in the midst of a busy life. The essential thing is to have some space of time — half an hour if possible, but at the very least a quarter — set apart every day for the purpose of prayer, in silence and solitude, and to remain faithful to that. You can find God in the midst of a busy life, but not if you never for a moment withdraw your mind from its business and wait upon Him.

Those who are filled with zeal for activity for the world, but are tempted to dismiss the need for daily prayer as a luxury in such times of crisis as these, may learn a lesson from the story of Elijah. You remember how he, too, a man of tremendously powerful personality and filled with zeal to triumph over God's enemies — but to triumph by a harsh display of might and wrath and violence — had indeed triumphed. He had brought down fire from Heaven upon his offering and slew the idolaters of Baal, and he was jubilant, thinking he had served God well. But then he saw his triumph turn to

ashes and was forced to flee for his life. And in his hu-
miliation and self-contempt, he threw himself down under a juniper tree and begged God that he might die,
because he was no better than his fathers. And God
vouchsafed him a vision, and showed him why his success had turned to failure.

First there came a great wind, which overthrew the
mountains and broke the rocks in pieces, but the Lord
was not in the wind; and then there came an earthquake, but the Lord was not in the earthquake; and then
there came a fire, but still the Lord was not there. But
after all these symbols of wrath and might and terror,
there came the whisper of a gentle wind, or, as another
version has it, the sound of a still, small voice; and when
the prophet heard it, he covered his head with his mantle for he knew that this was the Lord.[12]

This vision was to teach Elijah, first, that you cannot
fight for a merciful, gentle God without the weapons of
a merciful, gentle God; but perhaps we may see in it a
further symbolism. For this zeal without wisdom, this
determination to fight for God without understanding

[12]3 Kings 18:36-40, 19:1-4, 11-13 (RSV = 1 Kings 18:36-
40, 19:1-4, 11-13).

the nature of God, is the very thing we shall do unless we set out to seek Him before we attempt to serve Him. And if we seek Him, we must seek, not in sound and fury, but in the deep silence in which alone His voice can be heard.

But the ability to hear, the ability to open the mind to God, is something that can be won only by constant and regular effort. That is why you must have your time set apart for prayer every day,[13] and why you must refuse to be discouraged by an apparent lack of progress or by dryness, however persistent, and lack of devout emotions. The only practical test of the value of your prayer is whether it makes you more eager to do God's will. You have to find the type of prayer that is best suited to you

---

[13]You have to be prepared to give up even prayer, on occasion, at the call of charity; and sometimes there will be days when the half hour really is impossible. That is not necessarily a cause for worry unless such days begin to be frequent or turn into a whole succession of days. What is important is that the habit remain a habit, and even on the busiest days, a few minutes' recollection is always possible. Moreover, a fixed daily time for prayer is a useful help to forming the habit, but it need not be too rigid; and if we find it invaded by other calls upon us, we can usually, with a little forethought, find another time that will do as well.

individually. Some are best served at the beginning by a form of meditation, whether elaborate or simple, as a prelude and incentive to acts of adoration, sorrow, trust, love, and so on; others by simple aspirations which are themselves prayer, and can be repeated over and over again and mold the soul to their pattern.

You have to expect distractions and refuse to be dismayed or depressed by them. All that is required is that you go on, day by day, until God in His own time, if He wills it, calls you to other and higher forms of prayer and union with Him.

⌘

The Mass teaches us to pray

The second element in the life of prayer is the Liturgy. That is a thing in which we can all share, and must share. We may have neither time nor opportunity to take part in the Church's full liturgical cycle as you find it carried out in a Benedictine monastery, but we can all assist at Mass. No need to emphasize the primary importance of daily Mass: it is the substance, the foundation on which all the rest — the life of prayer and detachment — must be built. But we sometimes forget the importance also of the Liturgy as such.

Strive for union with God

To take part in the Mass, to say the words of the Mass with the priest and perform the appropriate gestures and movements, is to let the Church teach us to pray. It teaches us, first of all, to pray with body and mind alike, to make our entire personality an offering of worship. It lifts our prayer into a higher level and intensity of being, by embodying it in the total prayer of the Church and Her Head. And because it can mold us gradually, by its deep and varied appeal to senses and feeling, mind and heart, into conformity with the attitude of adoring self-offering which its symbolism expresses, it can lead us to the life of prayer in the fullest sense.

Thus it not only makes it easier to find in our times of mental prayer a real communion with God, but it also turns our whole lives, with all they contain, into a continuous act of worship and offering, and so transforms us gradually into beings of praise, which is indeed our destiny.

We should awaken ourselves to God's presence
This leads us to consider the third element in the life of prayer, which is precisely the habitual sense of the

presence of God. Here again you have to be prepared for a long and arduous struggle, and indeed, without the Liturgy and the daily time of prayer, it would be an impossibility. It does not mean, of course, that you have to be all the time consciously thinking of God: you have your work to do; you have to concentrate on other things. It does mean that you have to acquire the habit of constantly turning back to God, to the realization of His presence, both as present everywhere by His immensity and as dwelling within the soul as the object of love and knowledge through the supernatural gift of grace.

The first step is to learn to make use of odd moments of leisure to think of God, to be conscious of Him, and to speak to Him; and again, without trying to do violence to the mind by a rigid control, to spend some of the freedom which manual work affords in a simple form of prayer.

Similarly you have to remind yourself, from time to time, that the materials of your work and play and all your daily life are hallowed by the presence of Infinity within them and about them. And while, where beautiful things are concerned, you remember that it is the love of God that makes them lovely, you have to remember also that He and His love are present also in the weak and the mean and the ugly. But always, lest you fall into a woolly and sentimental sort of pantheism, you have to remember that the God who is thus present in the things He has made is the same God whom, in your prayers, you are learning to know and to worship — the Infinite Transcendent.

And then, if you go on faithfully making these acts of adoring awareness of God's presence, they will become habitual to you, and the sense of this presence will become natural to you, so that in the end, even when you are concentrating on other matters, it will never be wholly lost to you.[14]

Then you will be at least beginning to have within you the heart of Christ, for you cannot live habitually in His presence without habitually judging and willing in His presence. Thoughts and desires will tend more and more to be referred to Him and determined by Him, until, in the end, you have that fullness of life which is wisdom in the mind and holiness in the will. Mind and will are made wholly one with the True and the Good,

[14]See that charming and valuable little treatise *The Practice of the Presence of God*, by Brother Lawrence (c. 1605-1691; Carmelite lay brother and mystic).

and therefore able, like Catherine, to love the whole world and work for it even unto death.

Detachment is a proper love of creatures
The ideal of living always in God's presence can provide us with a clue to the next point we have to consider, the Christian doctrine called detachment. For if we live always in God's sight and try to act always according to His will, our attitude toward created things will necessarily come to be modeled on His.

The name *detachment* is indeed an unfortunate one: it sounds negative and niggardly, and can give rise to serious misunderstanding. Perhaps we should do well to speak rather of poverty of spirit, or indeed quite simply of the right love of creatures. For detachment is not a denial of life, but a denial of death; not a disintegration, but the condition of wholeness; not a refusal to love, but the determination to love truly, deeply, and fully.

Let us state the thing first in terms of the apparent contradiction with which the Gospel presents us. We have already been thinking of these words of our Lord: "By this shall men know that you are my disciples, that

you have love one for another."[15] And when He gives
His followers the two great commandments of love —
of God and of men — He tells them that the second
one is like unto the first.[16] Yet it was our Lord, too, who
said at another time, "If any man come to me and hate
not his father and mother and sister and brother, he
cannot be my disciple."[17] Can these opposing statements be reconciled?

There would be no opposing statements were it not
for the fact of sin, which gives an ambiguity to the way
we use the word *love*. Too often we say "love" when we
mean merely self-love: we say we love this or that, but we
mean simply that we like the pleasure these things can
give us; with their own well-being we are not concerned.
And to treat thus the things that God has made, our
fellow creatures, is to offend Him, for the love with
which He made them makes them lovable in themselves. But more than that, to treat things simply as
means to our own pleasure is to assume over them a dominion that is not ours; to try, in the last resort, to be

[15]John 13:35.
[16]Matt. 22:39.
[17]Luke 14:26.

as gods,[18] and so to refuse to obey God's will rather than our own.

Real love, on the other hand, is expressed in the words of the old definition, to will another's good, which implies that we allow no hardship or sacrifice to deter us from helping those we love. We look always to what is best for *them*, we love them therefore not as mere means to our pleasure, but as ends in themselves, as beings whom it is a joy and a privilege to serve. But to love them for themselves, for what they really are, is to love them as God's creatures, whose first duty is to Him; and therefore, while selfish covetousness turns creatures into God's rivals, because it tries to arrogate to itself their creaturely relationship to God, real love is *based upon* that relationship: it wills the good of the one loved, but it knows that that good is to be found in loving obedience to the will of God.

The love which is really only pride and covetousness, then, is incompatible with the love of God; real love, on the contrary, is a part of the love of God. And so, if we think of pride and covetousness as love, then, before we can be Christ's disciples, we must reverse our

[18]Cf. Gen. 3:5.

whole attitude: we must hate. If, on the other hand, we understand love aright, then indeed we are to rest assured that it will be through that love that we shall be known as His disciples.

We must speak, then, of a false love and a true, and whereas true love is not only permitted but commanded, false love is the stuff of all sin, for it is egoism, and egoism is rooted in pride, which is the primal sin. Egoism says, in effect, that anything that attracts you is your creature and you can do what you like with it; the power of decision, to do this or that, rests with you. In other words, you are committing the sin of self-idolatry, you are denying the absolutes of truth and goodness, and you are making yourself your own god. The thing can be seen at its crudest in those sins of rapacious greed for pleasure in which human beings treat one another as toys.

We are less ready to realize that the same is true, substantially, of those sins in which there is true love of another human being, but in which nonetheless we flout the will of God and make ourselves the arbiters of good and evil. In these, too, there is the same essential sin, for it is still the human judgment which is deified, and the divine which is denied.

Heart of Compassion

Sometimes indeed this problem will present itself in terms of an unbearable tension between the claims of a true human love and obedience to God: all one's instincts and feelings, all one's judgment and deep desire for another's good will rise up and cry out, "I cannot do this. I cannot cause all this suffering and all this harm for the sake of a principle." Then you have to try to remember that in fact we just do not know with any certainty what, in the long view, is for another's good; we just cannot foresee the consequences of our actions; we just do not understand the depths of the problem of suffering; and the only thing we can do, if we want to be wise, is to trust in the judgments of God. You remember the words of Job: "Even though He slay me, yet will I trust Him."[19] There may be times when you will have to say, "Even though He slay my friend, my lover, or my country, yet will I trust in Him"— and continue to obey Him.

We must sometimes forego good things for God
But the false love is not only expressed in a self-willed choice of evil in defiance of the law of God. Detachment

[19]Job 13:15.

means much more than the avoidance of that. There is a second sort of choice, not of evil as against good, but of a thing good in itself as against what is God's will for you at any given moment. You may say there is nothing wrong in this action, this interest, or this possession, in itself, and you may be right. But it may not be God's will for you; it may not be part of your particular vocation. And then, if you insist on clinging to it, you are still committing the primal sin of pride and egoism; you are still making yourself the arbiter of what is right for you.

Here we are nearer the core of the doctrine of detachment, for whenever you say of anything, no matter what it may be, "I cannot do without that; I will not do without that; I am going to decide what I do with it or for it or because of it," you are clinging to something in defiance of God, and consequently, however unselfish, however noble, however pure your love of it may be, humanly speaking, it is still to that extent a false love; it is still keeping you from the total service of God.

And suppose you have at long last schooled yourself to put God's will first in everything, to let Him decide what you shall have and not have, do and not do. Does it follow that you have ceased to love the world of men and of things? On the contrary, it may well mean exactly the opposite; it may well mean that at long last you have really *started* to love them — to love *them* and not yourself. Perhaps you only now begin to realize that since you are not their master, they for their part are not just means but ends; they are to be loved in themselves. You will also find that *all* the things that God has made and that He loves are lovable, and not just those things which you would otherwise have found superficially attractive.

Above all, you will love not less, but infinitely more than before, because, when you have reached this degree of identity with the will of God, you will have been given the heart of Christ as Catherine was. And so you will love with a breadth and depth which no merely human love can encompass. You will find that there is nothing so small or so mean as to escape your love, and nothing for which you would not gladly bear, as Christ did, a redeeming cross.

⚛

Detachment purifies our love

Once you realize, then, that detachment means simply the destruction of the false love in order to give birth to the true, the danger of misunderstanding detachment disappears. So also does the apparent contradiction in those words of our Lord, "If any man come to me and hate not his father and mother and sister and brother, he cannot be my disciple." Long ago, St. Thomas Aquinas put the matter very simply and very clearly, by quoting the injunction to hate father and mother and adding that this means insofar as they turn us from God — insofar as the love is a false love and not a true.[20] But to understand the thing in theory is not the same, alas, as carrying it out in practice.

There is no holiness without tears. You have to kill in yourself the love that is wholly selfish, that uses things as mere means, for what you can get out of them. And that is hard enough, but it is only the beginning. You have to kill in yourself the pride that spoils a love that, as far as its created object is concerned, is true and generous enough, but will not acknowledge the dominion of God. And that is harder. You have to learn to acknowledge that dominion, not

---

[20]St. Thomas Aquinas (c. 1225-1274; Dominican philosopher, theologian, and Doctor of the Church), *Summa Theologica*, II-II, Q. 26, art. 2.

only when it is a choice between good and evil, not only when it is a choice between what is good in itself and what is God's will for you here and now, but also in the sense of being prepared and ready in heart to ac-knowledge and welcome it universally and without qual-ification in the future, no matter what calls it may make upon your generosity, no matter what crosses it may invite you to bear. And that is the hardest of all.

We must be ready to let go of everything for God
The English mystic Walter Hilton,[21] in his *Scale of Per-fection*, has some valuable passages which reveal the dif-ficulty of this poverty and freedom of spirit even when outwardly the world has been wholly renounced. He is writing to a hermit: she has forsaken riches and posses-sions and is shut in a dungeon, but has she forsaken covetousness? It is easier, he says, to forsake worldly possessions than to forsake the love of them. Perhaps her covetousness remains with her, but it is changed from great things to small. It is a shrewd hit at the dan-ger which besets those who embrace a life of voluntary

---

[21]Walter Hilton (died 1396).

poverty — the danger of clinging to little valueless things with all the tenacity of a miser clutching his hoard.

But in any case, even if you were reduced to owning absolutely nothing, you could still fail to have detachment and freedom of spirit, for you could still hanker after the things you lacked; you could want them as your own, apart from God, and the lack of them could be more of a hindrance to the perfect love and service of God than ever the possession would have been.

These things are best seen in an example. There is someone you love very much: does detachment bid you to cease loving him? No, of course not, but it bids you to be sure that the love is true and not false, real love and not just covetousness. It bids you to learn to see the love as God's gift, not as your own property; as part of your vocation, and not as an escape from it. More than that, it bids you to leave your possession and enjoyment of it wholly in His hands.

Suppose you want to see the person you love, but God intervenes and prevents you. You must not rebel or try to circumvent His will. You must not grumble or think yourself ill-treated, nor must you brood upon your injuries. The thing is not yours, anyway, but His, and you must try to be ready to say, not of each particular incident as it arises, but of your love as a whole, "Even though He take it wholly from me, I will trust Him."

⚘

Seeking Heaven is woman's essential vocation
Our purpose in these meditations is to think of the vocation of woman in the world. But here you have the essential condition of all work, and of every vocation, in the world. You cannot work for God in the world unless you love the world. But you cannot love the world truly unless you have learned, or at least are learning day by day, to love God above all and all things in God, unless you have learned to live the life of prayer and of poverty of spirit.

"Seek ye first the kingdom of Heaven." This does not mean that you must seek only your own sanctification and forsake your responsibilities to the world. And it does not mean that you must reduce your love of created things to a thin, colorless, superficial likeness of detached benevolence. Rather, it means exactly the contrary. The more you love God, the more you will love the world, because the more you will share in His love of it. The more you can kill in yourself the false love that values things only for what you can get out of them, the more you will see them and love them as they really are. The more you rid yourself of possessiveness and pride, and free yourself of the slavery that ties you down to your possessions and the haunting dread of losing them, the greater your love will grow in breadth and in intensity until, in the end, it embraces, like the love of God, the whole of the sin-laden and suffering world.

St. Catherine exemplifies wisdom and detachment
When we think, then, of St. Catherine of Siena as of a leader and guide in whose footsteps we are to follow, let us salute in her first of all her *prayer*: the one thing necessary, the substance of life, from which action, if it is to be Christlike and redeeming, must, and will inevitably, flow. Let us salute in her, secondly, her *wisdom*: it was a wisdom that she learned in prayer — not the acquired wisdom of a powerful intellect, but the infused wisdom of a humble heart, the intuitive grasp of truth, the love-knowledge, which, as we shall see later, is the wisdom most proper to woman's vocation in the world. Let us salute in her, finally, the third condition without which no Christlike action is possible: her poverty and

freedom of spirit, her *detachment*. We are told that after her mysterious exchange of hearts with Christ she always prayed, not, "Lord, I offer Thee my heart," but, "Lord, I offer Thee *Thy* heart."

We have to remind ourselves that out of the long and laborious struggle with its three stages — the struggle to choose God's will instead of evil, to choose God's will instead of what is good in itself but not His will for us, and to choose God's will universally and without reservation, no matter what the future may bring, in an act of total self-offering — there comes the glory of possessing the heart of Christ, with all its immensity of divine and universal love, and all its immensity of power to heal and help the suffering world.[22]

---

[22] Detachment explains also the two ways in which the Bible speaks of the world. St. John tells us, "Love not the world"(1 John 2:15). He means the abode of mammon, the spirit of worldliness which rejects God and makes its own god of money or power or pleasure. That is egoism, the false love. But he also tells us, "God so loved the world as to give His Son to save it" (cf. John 3:16-17); and that world is the earth and its fullness, His handiwork, and especially the race of men, His children. To love that world as such is part of man's love of God, the true love.

If we try, slowly and painfully but doggedly, to follow in Catherine's footsteps and seek first, as she did, the kingdom of Heaven, then we need have no fear that our efforts to serve the world will be frustrated or end in failure. For we shall more and more fully express in our lives His will and His redeeming love; we shall share in the desire of His heart and in His power to fulfill it; and we shall not worry about the results of our work — the success or failure that the future may bring — because we shall become more and more content to do what He tells us. And in the end the rest will be added unto us.

�£

Nurture the maternal
qualities in your soul

*His mother kept all these
words in her heart.*

Luke 2:51

❦

"The head cannot say to the feet, 'I have no need of you.'"[23] Christ needs the members of His Mystical Body[24] to carry out His redemptive work in the world; that we have already considered. But you remember how Pope Pius XII, in his encyclical *Mystici Corporis*, is at pains to stress the fact already pointed out by St. Paul, that different members have by definition different functions to fulfill according to their different gifts. And if you hold that grace perfects nature, takes what we are by nature and makes that the material of the supernaturalized life, then you must hold also that the differences of natural as well as of supernatural gifts determine the

[23] Cf. 1 Cor. 12:21.
[24] The "Mystical Body" refers to the collective members of the Church, with Christ as the Head. Cf. 1 Cor. 12:27; Col. 1:18.

function that the Christian is to fulfill in the Church. That is the basis of the Christian doctrine of vocation.

⚜

Man and woman have different vocations
Now, underneath all the varieties of individual qualities and characteristics, there lies the greatest of all natural differentiations: that between man and woman. It is true that we are none of us wholly male or female in our makeup; but it remains permissible to speak of the male mind or the female mind, and therefore of the vocation of man and the vocation of woman, inasmuch as there are some qualities of mind and soul which ought to be predominant in man, and others which ought to be predominant in woman. Let me add that very great people, the genius and the saint, seem to stand above these differentiations and to unite in themselves, in creative harmony, the qualities of both sexes; and we all have to try to be saints, so that for all of us, the ideas we have to consider are bound to be ultimately relevant.

"His mother kept all these words in her heart." This text gives us a clue to the essence of the matter. If you look at primitive societies, where human nature is at its simplest, you find a clear-cut division: the man is the breadwinner, the active one, and the builder; the woman is the housewife, the receptive one, and the conserver. It is the man who goes out to hunt; the woman stays behind to preserve the home and the family. And as the intellectual life of a community evolves, the same fundamental distinction persists: it is the man, the builder and legislator, who represents reason; and the woman, the conserver and consoler, who represents intuition. The man adventures in ideas, in science and philosophy, and builds up what is new; the woman conserves the deep, lasting, unchanging wisdom in her heart.

You hear a great deal nowadays about the equality of the sexes: there is a great danger here. If you are trying to defend woman from the degradation of being treated as a chattel, from the horrors of child-marriage and so on, then of course you are wholly right; these things are a crime against human nature and against the laws of God. But be careful: if by *equality*, you mean an obliteration of the difference between the sexes, you will end by destroying the integrity of both. For the whole idea and purpose of the difference is that the two together are complementary: they complete one another precisely because they differ from one another. Man and woman are meant to have the equality of true companionship, but true companionship does not exclude a subordination on one plane.

If we had begun this meditation with some of the sayings of St. Paul about woman, would you have been irritated or depressed? If you had been either, you would have been wrong. You will not achieve the freedom and dignity of woman by trying to turn her into a man; you will only destroy her, and man as well.

On one level, there is a subordination, there is obedience. But be comforted: on another level, it is woman who indisputably reigns. Her special role, spiritually and intellectually, as well as biologically and economically, is just as necessary to man as his is to her. They are partners, fellow workers, and you ruin everything if you try to give them both the same work.

Woman brings special understanding to family life
St. Paul tells us that it is only when Christ dwells in the heart that we may hope to comprehend with the saints the length and breadth and height and depth, so as to be filled with all the fullness of God.[25] It is the destiny of

[25]Cf. Eph. 3:18-19.

every Christian, since every Christian is called to become a saint; but it has a special relevance to woman's vocation. For it is this sense of length and breadth and height and depth that she in particular — because of her natural gifts first of all — is meant to bring to the human family. Man, the rational, active builder, tends to be concerned with the immediate and apparent needs of life, with the surface, and in consequence tends to take the short view; woman is meant by nature to be slower to leap to conclusions. It is for her to keep in her heart the words and the experiences which life brings to them both and, having kept them in her heart, to come to understand them in a different way.

She must know the length: she must be able to take a long view, not so much rationally as intuitively; she must see beyond the immediate necessities and advantages, and sense ultimate effects.

She must know the breadth: it is easy for the man, all too easy, in the struggle for life, to find himself involved in facile enmities. It is for her to preserve in herself and in him the sense of the unity of the human family and indeed of all the creatures of God.

She must know the height. It is easy for the man to become so wrapped up in his human work and human striving for progress that he comes to measure all things by purely human standards, or at least forgets that there are things that matter even more than daily bread. She must preserve his human labors along the horizontal line of human progress from the dangers of shallowness and perhaps idolatry by her upward, vertical striving of spirit toward divinity. She must be always bringing back a humanist world to the sense of God.

She must know the depth. It is her heaviest cross and her greatest glory. The humanist world is a shallow world, a world of false and facile optimism, inasmuch as it forgets the fact of sin, or tries to ignore it. But you cannot ignore the underworld of life with impunity. Either you must go down into it, suffer it, understand it, and overcome it; or you can try to forget it for a time, and then, sooner or later, it will rise up against you and destroy you.

And when a whole civilization tries thus to forget the sense of depth, it may live very placidly on the surface for a while; it may make immense progress, but still on the surface; and then its nemesis will come upon it, and it will find itself driven back to the darkness of the caves. That is why, even on a purely natural reckoning, we so desperately need the vocation of woman in the world today, and why we need so desperately this aspect of the fullness of life of the saints.

Mary is the model of the vocation of woman
Let us think, then, of the woman who most perfectly and most completely fulfilled the vocation of woman: the Mother of God. We may remind ourselves, first of all, in view of what we were thinking about before, that she was fit to be the mother because she was fit to be the bride, and she was fit to be the bride because she makes her *fiat* absolute and unconditional: "Behold the handmaid of the Lord; be it done to me according to thy word."[26] That identity of will with the will of God, which we were thinking of before as the condition of all Christlike action in the world, is here the condition of the coming of Christ Himself into the world. Eve, the mother of mankind, had brought evil into the world through self-will, through setting her own will in opposition to the will of God; Mary, the mother of redeemed mankind, brought the Savior into the world by reversing the primal sin, by identifying her will utterly

[26]Luke 1:38.

with the will of God, and by fulfilling once again in its entirety the essential destiny of the human soul — to be the handmaid of the Lord.

But in what sense is she the mother of mankind, the universal mother? First of all, she gives birth to the new race, the new world, through her Son, in whom the world is renewed. Secondly, a mother is always in-volved in the work and destiny of her son; and the work of Mary's Son is the Redemption of the race of men. Thirdly, her acceptance of her destiny is at the same time an acceptance, on behalf of humanity, of the spir-itual marriage between humanity and divinity, brought about first of all in the person of Christ and thence, through and in Him, although in a different sense, in all who believe in His name and do His will.

Motherhood is present in the heart of every woman
Mary is the universal mother, and that very fact is in it-self one of the reasons why she is the supreme type of womanhood. There is an element of motherhood in ev-ery love that is true and deep, and that is at the very center of the vocation of woman. Having learned with Mary to say, "Behold the handmaid of the Lord," you

must then go on to imitate her in this above all, if your proper vocation in the world is to be fulfilled.

The rational mind of the male tends to take the short view, to become involved in rivalries and enmities, to ignore the heights of the eternal hills and the depths of evil and misery; and for any or all of these reasons, the rational schemes of the male and all his work of building and all his ambitions tend to come tumbling down, sooner or later, in ruins about him. It is then that woman is meant to find her vocation as mother of man, and her share in the universal motherhood of Mary. Sometimes indeed it is only this catastrophe which can enable her to recall man to the sense of length and breadth and height and depth. When all goes well, he refuses to listen; he meets her wisdom with a parade of logic and beats it down. It is not until he has seen his own world crashing about him, seen the chaos to which he has brought himself, that he comes back to be reborn in the womb of her compassion and realizes belatedly that she was right; realizes perhaps that all the time he knew unconsciously that she was right and that his parade of reason was only an escapist mechanism of rationalization.

But she for her part will throw away her destiny if, in the moments of failure and abjection, she despises him;

if she does that, she fails herself. She has to preserve her faith in him, and she has to preserve his own faith in himself, in his ability to start again, to rebuild in a new spirit what is broken or to build something new and more worthwhile.

❧

A wife can share in her husband's vocation

Here she may have to meet her greatest temptation, in this moment when her essential vocation is fulfilled. It is the temptation to make herself the triumphant rival of the work the man is meant to do. Not that the temptation is confined to these moments, but it is here that it can be most acute.

Think of the normal evolution of the married life of a man and a woman. They marry because they love each other; but they marry in order that together they may build something other than themselves: the family. In other words, the man is not only to be husband, but also father; the woman is not only to be wife, but also mother. Their glory is to share together as ministers of God's omnipotence in the making of new immortal beings, and to help them to grow up in God's likeness and lead them safely to God. But they have to learn not only that that is God's will for them, but also, sometimes, that that is the perfect fulfillment of their love. And sometimes the lesson is a hard one. Sometimes they can be tempted to resent their destiny as a distraction from their love, to go on forever being lovers and escaping the responsibilities of being makers. If they do that, they will never have the fullness of life or the fullness of love; they will never grow up.

The temptation for the woman is twofold.

The man has his home and his career, and he may neglect one of them for the sake of the other. The woman, for her part, may be tempted to view his career either as a rival, withdrawing him from her, or at least as a part of his life in which she has no share. In either case, she fails to fulfill her destiny. For it is no longer his career, his work; it is their career, their work. She is dependent on him, on the results of his work, so that the home may be preserved; but he, for his part, is dependent on her — on the wisdom she can bring him if she has learned her destiny aright, on her faith in him, and on her love and the strength it gives her to support them and give them hope in times of crisis and distress. She has to learn her particular wisdom, her particular work. She has to learn the particular qualities she needs as a

wife, precisely in order to help him achieve his vocation and to share in his work. Every Christian has to
think of the work God has given him to do as being
more important than his own well-being; she has to
think this of the work God has given her *in her husband*.

But it may happen that he, for his part, becomes so
absorbed in his career that he loses interest in her, and
it may be only failure that will bring him back. And it
is when that happens that she has to meet the keenest
temptation — the temptation to spend all her energies
simply on retaining his love permanently instead of giving him new heart for his work. She must, of course,
want to retain his love, but she must try to reintegrate
his life, not destroy a part of it. Her vocation is still to
minister to the work, and if she does that, it is surely
probable that her faith and love and strength will themselves win back for her the fullness of his love; whereas
if she sets herself up as a rival, she will at best only triumph for a time, for you cannot frustrate half of a man's
nature indefinitely.

That is her first temptation.

The second comes of the duality of her life as wife
and mother. When she is first married, perhaps the man's
predominant attitude will be one of adoration; she will

be in a position to command. The power that sex gives you over another's will is a terrible thing: it can be used to teach and to save, but it can also be used to destroy and to ruin. Her temptation will be to preserve that relationship unchanged; to preserve at all costs the power, and therefore the endowments which give the power. And again, if she does that, she will be throwing away not only his destiny, but her own.

Devotion to the family creates deep love and unity
A woman cannot create a family or a home unless she loves her children completely, but she cannot love them completely unless, feeling their dependence on her, she gives herself entirely to them. That is why she has to stop being a goddess on a pedestal and become a worker in a kitchen and a nursery. And one day the man will realize that his wife is not a goddess, but a hard-worked woman, beginning to show signs of the work and worry she has had to contend with. And then — and it is part of *his* growth to fullness — he should be moved with compassion to think that it is her devotion to him and to his children that has brought about this change. He should be filled with a sense of his family's dependence

on him, and a determination to take care of it and provide for it and cherish it, cost what it may. And if the man and woman both accept their vocation in this way, in the fullness of the demands it makes on them, then they learn a deeper love and unity than ever they could achieve in the more lyrical and idyllic stage of their career: they fulfill in their lives the image of the Holy Family.

"Mary kept all these words in her heart." It is Joseph who has to make the decisions; and to whom the angel speaks when they are to escape into Egypt.[27] It is Joseph who provides and protects and compassionates. But you cannot imagine the life at Nazareth without imagining the wisdom, the perhaps often unspoken wisdom, he learned from Mary, as well as the protective love and compassion with which she, too, in her different way, surrounded him, and her identification of herself with the work he had to do.

But above all, you cannot imagine the life at Nazareth apart from the complete self-dedication of Joseph and Mary alike to the work, the vocation, of their Son. He advanced in wisdom and age and grace with God and

[27]Matt. 2:13.

men, St. Luke tells us;[28] and it was under the tutelage of Joseph and Mary, for we are told also that He went down with them and came to Nazareth and was subject to them.[29]

And when it was time for His public work, His mother, who had prepared Him for it, so far from detaining Him, seemed to efface herself, to disappear from the picture. But her heart was in Him and in His work, and if she disappeared, it was only to reappear when He needed her; to be there at the end, in her faith and love and courage, to share His cry of dereliction, and to hear Him say, "It is perfected."[30]

All women share in Mary's universal motherhood
Mary, the Queen of the Seven Swords,[31] knew as no other woman has known the length and breadth and height and depth. It is not only married women, it is all women who have to share, in their degree, her vocation

28Luke 2:52.
29Luke 2:51.
30Cf. John 19:30.
31See Gerald Vann, *At the Foot of the Cross* (Manchester, New Hampshire: Sophia Institute Press, 1998).

of the motherhood of man, and to share it by sharing her wisdom.

She knew the length, she who was told so early on: "Thy own soul a sword shall pierce;"[32] seeing in her Child's play the future Passion, and seeing — sensing in her heart — in the Passion the glory of the Redemption.

She knew the length because she knew, she saw in her Son's story, that immediate failure is often ultimate success, and apparent success is often ultimately failure; she knew that what is wisdom to men is often folly to God.[33] And those who share in her vocation have to share in her length of view: theirs is the majesty of bringing up souls for God, their eyes fixed not on the immediate and often illusory objectives of money and social advancement, but on the ultimate objective of the fullness of eternal life.

And their work is like the work of the precursor, John the Baptist, who sent his disciples away from him to follow their true destiny when the Master came: they have to wean their children — spiritually as well as physically — teach them to be independent, and give

[32]Luke 2:35.
[33]1 Cor. 3:19.

them to the world. And although they remain with
their children, to support them in the background, as
Mary remained to the end at the foot of the Cross, it
must be only to help them to do better the work they
have to do. And this is a role that belongs to all who
share the vocation of woman — not only to wives and
to mothers of families. It belongs to all those who work
for the world, even quite apart from the personal rela-
tionships that this may involve. There is always the
need of bringing the wisdom of the long view to any
enterprise, lest it start in a glitter of easy optimism, but
rapidly end in failure and despair.

This role belongs in particular to the women of
prayer in the Church, for it is their prayer life which
supports the Church's activity and those responsible
for it. It is these women who stand behind the mission-
ary enterprises, for example, and give them the power
to continue undismayed; it is they who stand behind all
the activity which attempts to incarnate the truth of
God in the material of earthly life, to preserve it from
becoming immersed in immediate issues and to give it
a sense of its final end.

Mary, the mother of men, knew the breadth, precisely because of the universality of her love and her

motherhood, precisely because she loves all that her Son loves. And the role of women in the world — countering the tendency of men to be immersed in their immediate partisanships and to forget the unity of the human family — makes it especially urgent for them to have within them the heart of Christ and its universality, and in particular to have a sense of the unity of the Mystical Body. In these days above all, when the world is torn by conflict and by hatred, and the hope for the unity of the world seems no more than an idle dream, we need this aspect of woman's gift to the world.

We know the words of our Lord: "You have heard that it hath been said, 'Thou shalt love thy neighbor and hate thy enemy.' But I say to you, love your enemies, do good to them that hate you . . . that you may be the children of your Father who is in Heaven."[34] We know the words, but we fail to fulfill them. But woman has, even biologically, a relationship to the race as a whole quite different from that of man. Its story is recapitulated in her womb, and she knows it in the helplessness of infancy, in the crudities of the fundamental needs and desires in which all men are one; and that

[34]Matt. 5:43-45.

gives her a special knowledge and a special responsibility — and she has to learn to see in every human being not only the humanity, but the divinity, the presence of God which is in them all, and the divine destiny in which they all share. So she must join with Mary in throwing the mantle of her care over all the human family; and then she will join with Mary also in bringing that family back to God.

Woman must raise man's vision to eternal truths
Mary, the Tower of Ivory, knew the height. You find her first with her hands and eyes uplifted to the message of God made known to her by the angel. You find on her lips the greatest and loveliest of all boasts — "Behold from henceforth all generations shall call me blessed"[35] — but because she is simply and humbly stating a fact, the fact of a glory which comes from God and which she trembles to receive, her eyes are again fixed not on herself, but on Him who is mighty and hath done great things to her.[36] And you find her again

[35]Luke 1:48.
[36]Luke 1:49.

at the end, standing by the Cross, and again her eyes are uplifted to the Figure upon it; for you do not read that she, the Tower of Ivory, was weeping. Even the horror of the final sword does not cause her to flinch from her faith and her courage, nor to forget that what is folly and failure to men is wisdom and redemption in the eyes of God.

She knew the height: she who, when she cuddled her Child, knew that He was also her God, so her life of devotion to the work of her Son was at the same time, in itself, a life of devotion to her Lord. She knew the height: she whose every action was a preparation for, or a sharing in, the work of redemption, and whose knowledge of the ways and purposes of God was far removed from the worldly-mindedness of those who thought to find in the Messiah a rebuilder of their lost political independence.

Those who share her vocation have here again a special duty today, when so much sincere desire to improve the lot of humanity is vitiated by its inability to measure what is for the good of man by reference to eternal truth. The humanist world is roofed in low by its self-imposed limitations, and stifles men who, perhaps without knowing it, long for a sight of the infinite skies.

And its programs of social reform are apt to end in arrogance, because they lack the dimension of worship, and in a progressive mechanizing and regimenting of human nature itself, because they fail to realize that the endless upward striving of humanity is not in the last resort toward material ends, however beneficent, but toward the supernatural destiny of the sons of God.

Woman must have compassion for the world
Finally, it is as Refuge of Sinners and Comforter of the Afflicted that we salute the Mother of God; for she, beyond all other women, knew the dimension of depth. If a woman insists on trying to make her life with a man a perpetual honeymoon and nothing more, she will never know the ultimate greatness and the ultimate depths of love and oneness with which her motherhood might have adorned her.

If you think of our Lady only as the maiden who is makeless[37] or as the Queen of Heaven, you will only know a part of her. You will miss the sublimity, and the

---

[37]*O Holy Night!* "I sing of a maiden," (Manchester, New Hampshire: Sophia Institute Press, 1995), 33.

pathos and the nearness, of the Mother of Sorrows. It is because she suffered in such closeness to her Son that she has, more than any other woman, an understanding of the sins and the sorrows of the world, and a greater share than any other woman in the wisdom and the compassion of Christ.

If you want to know the depths, you have to study the problem of pain and of evil, not with the brain merely, but with the heart. The length must give you a sense of the immeasurable chain of evils that sin begets. The breadth must show you the immensity of the world's sin and give you a sense of your share in it, a feeling of responsibility for it because it weighs down on the shoulders of the members of your family. The height must reveal to you the density of sin's darkness against the flawless purity of the white-hot fire of God's love. But all this will flare up into life within you only when you yourself have learned to suffer in your own heart the sorrows of others, and to feel in your own heart the reality of sin.

We have been thinking of the way in which a woman can find her destiny at the very moment when man has failed. But without the sense of depth, she will miss it because she will despise him for his failure, and everything will be lost. "Mary kept all these words in her heart": she had to gain her understanding of the depths through her deep penetration of the mind and heart of God. With us the case is different; there are things we can see all too clearly in ourselves.

Mary had to learn of the sin of man and the mercy of God when she saw and suffered what men did to her Son, and heard His prayer to the Father to forgive them[38] — we are ourselves among them. But our experiential knowledge of evil is worse than useless to us unless we acquire, or rather can become worthy to be given, the ability to see it as Mary did, through the eyes of God.

St. Teresa[39] tells us that as a soul progresses toward God, there comes a time when the sense of its own sin, as set against the majesty and purity and love of God, becomes an unbearable burden. It is just that awareness, the fruit of many prayers and many trials, that we need above all in the world today. It is out of the womb of divine compassion, of the love that emptied itself of

[38]Luke 22:34.
[39]St. Teresa of Avila (1515-1582), Spanish Carmelite nun, mystic, and Doctor of the Church.

infinity to take on the form of a man, that redemption is born; and it is insofar as woman can share in that love and that compassion that she, too, can fulfill her essential work.

Woman can foster unity and peace through love
There can be no peace in the world, and therefore no renewal, except by the restoration of the world's unity. But its unity will never be restored by the violent and external regimentations of collectivism; it can be restored only by a recovery of a personal consciousness of unity on the part of individual human beings. There is the unselfconscious unity of a primitive tribe: we must neither revert to that nor desire to revert to it. There is the disintegration of an individualist civilization, and that has brought us to our present pass. There is no way out for us except the effort to establish consciously a conscious unity, a conscious family life, which is the same as saying that peace is the fruit of charity. And here, too, you have a clear expression of the vocation of woman.

If you think of the great women who have altered, or have labored to alter, the face of our civilization —

Elizabeth Fry,[40] Florence Nightingale,[41] Nurse Edith Cavell,[42] Catherine of Siena, or Teresa of Avila — you always seem to find that they are fighting for the inner values, the deeper values, which alone make the fulfillments of male ambition bearable. Patriotism is not enough, justice is not enough, and scientific power is only a servant. The great women always recall us to the deeper needs and the greater destinies; and so they try to save the world from the shallow, the slick, the facile, and the cruel, and to show us that the world of men is not meant to be either a battlefield or a laboratory, but a family.

Keep the words of God, the things that God does, and the events and experiences that He sends you, in your heart; use them in prayer and sacrifice to increase your vision of the length and breadth and height and depth. Then, no doubt, you will share with Mary in the sorrows of the seven swords, but you will share with her also in the motherhood of man.

[40]Elizabeth Fry (1780-1845), Quaker prison reformer.
[41]Florence Nightingale (1820-1910), reformer of hospital nursing.
[42]Edith Cavell (1865-1915), English nurse during World War I.

And in the degree to which you can copy her humility — the humility of her "Behold the handmaid of the Lord" — you will share in her glory. You of your own smaller life and smaller world will be able to say something approaching the words with which she described her future glory in the world as a whole: "Behold from henceforth all generations shall call me blessed, for He who is mighty hath done great things in me, and holy is His name."

✣

Learn compassion

Carry me, Christ, on the Cross,
which is salvation for the wanderers,
sole rest for the wearied, wherein
alone is life for those who die.

St. Ambrose

⚜

As we know from St. Paul, it is an essential part of the Christian life that we should make up what is wanting in the sufferings of Christ, in our flesh, for His body, which is the Church.[43] And we have seen how Pope Pius XII, in *Mystici Corporis*, explains the way in which the Head needs the members for the fulfillment of His work. It is not that there is any lack of power in Him, but it is His will that the power should reach men through the agency of the Church, so in fact the salvation of many depends on the prayers and penances that Christians offer to God for this intention. And Pope Pius is at pains to emphasize that this sharing in the redemptive work of Christ as His instruments is not the prerogative and responsibility simply of the Church's

[43]Col. 1:24.

pastors: it is part of the life of every Christian and, he says, especially of fathers and mothers of families.

෯

St. Monica's tears led her wayward son to God

We cannot think adequately of woman's vocation within the Mystical Body of Christ without thinking of the mystery of vicarious suffering and expiation. It is also inseparable from the idea of Christian motherhood.

Let us think a little of the saint who has a special place in the Church's life as patroness, under our Lady, of married women and mothers, and who is the great exemplar of the glory of the vocation of tears: St. Monica (c. 331-387). Her married life was not an easy one. She had much to suffer from her husband, Patricius, especially from his violent rages; but her quiet strength and patience compelled him at least to respect her; and in the end, her prayers and her personality led him to Baptism and to a holy death. That was her first victory of vicarious expiation: the firstfruits of her tears. But it is for her sorrows over her son Augustine[44] that she is

---

[44]St. Augustine (354-430), Bishop of Hippo and Doctor of the Church.

famous, just as it is through them that she won her greatest victory for the Church.

Mother and son do indeed present that contrast between the sexes which we have been considering: Augustine, headstrong and wayward, ambitious, brilliant, making a career for himself, reasoning brilliantly but often wrongheaded; Monica, quiet, constant in her love, humbly standing in the background, following him where his ambition led him so as to be at hand, if occasion offered, to help him, keeping her own deeper wisdom in her heart, weeping over him but not nagging. Later on, when Augustine was preparing for Baptism at Cassiacum, Monica joined in their philosophical discussions, and they wondered at her wisdom. But it was not her tongue but her tears that converted him. The words of a bishop who comforted her in her distress are famous: "It cannot be that the child of these tears should perish."

༄

Tears can help to redeem our sinful world
Let us note, first of all, that we are right to speak of the mystery of *redemptive* tears. We are not concerned here simply with a natural sensibility. And of course we use the word *tears* to cover not only the sorrow, but the

prayers and the sufferings, the expiation, as well. We are concerned with the tears that express a deep feeling of responsibility in the sight of God, that are themselves a prayer and a sacrifice to God, and that are a part of the vocation of Christian motherhood because the love of the son who causes them is in itself an aspect of the love of God. It is tears such as these that can be the channel of saving grace; it is the children of tears such as these who cannot perish.

There are always wives or mothers — and more than ever perhaps in these present days — who find themselves in the same position as St. Monica, and the first lesson of her life is for them. It is a message of hope and encouragement: they need not despair because they cannot meet impiety or disbelief with weighty argument or brilliant logic — it is not these things alone, anyway, that change the heart of a man. They need only follow the example of St. Monica in her tears and her prayers, and leave the rest to the mercy of God.

But the lesson has a far wider application than that. Msgr. Bougaud,[45] at the end of his *Life of St. Monica*,

---

[45]Louis Victor Emile Bougaud (1823-1888), professor, writer, and Bishop of Laval.

thanks her, because in revealing her heart to him, she has taught him also to know his own. "Thanks to thy teaching," he says, "I know now better than I did before at what cost souls are to be ransomed, and that if a true mother must possess a priestly heart, the heart of a true priest must be a maternal one." For since it is part of the office of the priest to lead souls back to God, he cannot carry out his work unless he possesses the qualities of soul of a Monica. If he is hard and cold, if he lacks understanding of and sympathy for the struggles and temptations and weaknesses of human beings, he will never be able to do his work, however learned he may be in theology and eloquent in preaching.

Some indeed may be kept from the danger of an aloof superiority simply because of their consciousness of their own inability to achieve ordinary rectitude of conduct themselves, but they are not necessarily in a better case — a sense of one's own sin is not of much avail unless it is allied with the sense of God and the determination to learn more and more to think and to will with the heart of Christ.

And when you have both sympathy for your fellow sinners and identity of will with the will of God, you have what is required to fulfill the vocation, not only of wives and mothers of families, not only of priests, but of all who are called to share in the priesthood of Christ by a life of redemptive prayer and work and suffering in the world — and in particular, the life of Christian womanhood.

Let us think a little more of these two conditions. Augustine, speaking to God of the sorrow of his mother over his sins, and the tears she shed for them, says in the *Confessions,* "For she, through that faith and the spirit which Thou hast given her, saw my death; and Thou didst hearken to her, O Lord. Thou didst hearken to her, and didst not despise her tears when in streams they rolled down her cheeks on the ground wherever she prayed; Thou didst hearken to her."[46]

⁂

Tears are redemptive in two ways
Monica saw her son's death: that is the first thing. You cannot do this work if you have only an academic interest in the sins of the world. Monica saw her son's death; but she saw it as a death in her own heart; and so God hearkened to her tears.

[46]*Confessions,* Bk. 3, ch. 11.

Learn compassion

You have to learn to say *"De profundis"*[47] for the whole human family, not as something outside yourself but as something identified with yourself. You therefore have to learn first the sense of sin, and that means learning both to love God and to love and understand the world of men. And that in its turn means thinking long and deeply. It means keeping the words of life in your heart. It means, not trying to escape the cruelties and crudities of reality, but on the contrary, trying to enfold all the pain of the world in the arms of your compassion, and feeling responsible for the sin of men as a mother feels responsible for the sin of her son, and, as Augustine says again of his mother, travailing in birth with them as often as you perceive that they go astray from God.

The second condition is as important as the first. Monica led Patricius away from his vices and back to God; she did so, Augustine tells us, because she was able to reveal God to him by her virtues, in which God had made her beautiful. If you are to lead men, they must feel your understanding and sympathy; but if you are to lead men to God, they must sense in you the

[47]"Out of the depths"; Ps. 129 (RSV = Ps. 130).

presence of God. Those tears which spring from the heart of Christ within you are redemptive, and they are redemptive in a double sense.

There is first the mystery of vicarious expiation, even in some strange way of vicarious sorrow, in itself. Because the Church is a communion of saints, and a communion of sinners — a true Mystical Body in which all the members share a common life — it follows that the well-being of the whole body is enhanced by the holiness of individual members; and we have seen already how the prayers and penances of the faithful Christian are meant to be the channels whereby the saving grace of Christ comes to those in need. And it is not that you can expiate the sins of others only by prayer and penance: God hearkened to the *tears* of Monica. To bear the weight of the sins of others in your heart, as our Lord bore the sins of the world on the Cross, as the saints bear them because of their oneness with Him, is in itself a sacrifice which has the power to expiate, so that the tears seem themselves to freshen and quicken the arid soil of the world.

That is indeed the second sense in which they are redemptive. It is not only that they can *merit* for another the grace of sorrow and renewal. They themselves can be the *instrument* used by God for its bestowal, a part of the process of conversion.

We know how the words of Christ could change the whole heart of a man; perhaps we ought to think more of the power of the tears of Christ to change the heart of the world. He wept over Lazarus in the tomb,[48] and Lazarus was raised to life; surely it is permissible to see in this scene a symbol of the power of tears to quicken and restore. He wept over Jerusalem,[49] and surely it is right that we should remember it often in these days, when hatred and persecution of the Jewish race has cast so deep a stain on the soul of Europe,[50] and should see in it precisely the promise of the final Redemption of Israel of which St. Paul speaks.[51]

Can it be that the child of these tears should perish? It cannot, because the tears are an offering to God, on behalf of the child, of that sorrow which is the necessary condition of the return to God. It cannot, because the tears themselves may, in God's mercy, be the way in

---

[48]John 11:35.
[49]Luke 19:41.
[50]Fr. Vann is speaking of the treatment of Jews during World War II. — ED.
[51]Cf. Rom. 11:26.

which the heart of the child is softened again and made again receptive, and so prepared for grace.

The tears themselves are redemptive, but they lead beyond themselves, to the making up for what is wanting in the *sufferings* of Christ. Pope Pius XII, in the encyclical we have already been considering, tells us how Christ proved His love for the Church, not only by His labors and prayers, but also by His sorrows and sufferings, gladly and lovingly endured for the Church's sake. It was only with His blood that He purchased the Church. And we, for our part, are to try to do the same. For, he says, although our Lord's Passion and death merited for the Church an infinite treasure of grace, yet it is not God's will that these graces should be granted to us all at once; and the measure in which they are bestowed depends in no small part on the way in which we do penance in union with the sufferings of Christ, and accept humbly and gladly as He did the burdens and sorrows which life brings us.

We can purify our hearts through little sacrifices
This, then, is practical advice for those who wish to fulfill the vocation of woman in the world. There is first

of all bodily penance. We need not think of anything dramatic — and indeed the only safe rule where physical mortification is concerned is that it should be done only under the advice of a confessor. But there are all sorts of small, secret and, in themselves, insignificant ways in which the will can be trained in obedience to God through the training of the body.

Then there is the mortification of the spirit. Here you are on safer ground, for the mortification of the flesh needs to be limited, but there is no limit to the extent to which you can healthily curb idle curiosity, ill-temper, criticism of others, and so on.

Finally, and above all, there is the lifelong mortification of freely, gladly, and unconditionally accepting the will of God, not only at the present moment, but for the whole of the future, no matter what it may bring. And included in this acceptance is the act of worship which turns all sorrows and joys alike into the material of sacrifice — a sacrifice which can be for the salvation of many. Included in it also are the deep Christian joy which will not be cast down by misfortune or failure; the patience that, where the saving of the world is concerned, will never give in; and the love that will never grow tired.

⁂

The world needs redemptive tears

When you look at the world today, it is easy to despair. There is so much suffering, so much horror, and so much blank misery. Perhaps some of it touches you very closely, and you feel that your own suffering, because of it, is useless and helpless, and so there is no hint of hope in your heart that out of it all some good may come.

You must not think that. You must remember Monica and the vocation of tears. You must remember how the Pope, as he writes of the endless throng of suffering human beings passing before his eyes, bids them lift up their eyes in confidence to God. Let them all remember, he says, that their sufferings are not in vain; they will be great gain to them, and to the Church, if only they take courage and bear them patiently with that end in view.

You need not be desperate because you can do nothing to help those millions who have been overwhelmed by misery, because you can do nothing to stop the crimes and brutalities, the seemingly irremediable evils that are being wrought in the world today. By the fact that you suffer for them before God, and offer your suffering for them to God, you are already redeeming them. Out of evil, good can come: the condition is the shedding of redemptive tears.

Even apart from the special horrors and sins which the war has brought in its train, the world of today stands in urgent need of the tears of the lovers of God. It needs them precisely because of its lack of the sense of depth, of the sense of sin, of the sense of its need of God and its need of redemption. If you are willing to work and pray and suffer in order to restore to the world its sense of these things, then you are accepting a vocation whose importance you cannot exaggerate.

Without this we are lost. Without this we may have grandiose schemes of social betterment; we may achieve the abolition of many social evils and the distribution of many social benefits; we may be given a vast increase in material comforts; we may even find ourselves witnessing a renaissance of culture, but, in the end, they will all be only a distraction and turn to ashes in our mouths, unless first of all we learn to cry to God out of the depths. They will be a distraction as the progress made by scientific humanism has in fact been a distraction in the past; they will make the surface of life more comfortable and more pleasing, and so we shall forget that the realities of life are escaping us.

We shall forget in particular the underground world, or we shall do our best not to think of it. And so we shall still be modern man in search of a soul — unconsciously searching, consciously trying to pretend there is nothing to search for. And then in the end once again the underworld will break forth, and we shall be powerless to control it, and there will be more chaos and more horror and more misery and more accumulation of evil.

❧

Sorrow is essential to the life of the Church

This vocation of tears is not a luxury in the Church's life. There are vocations which bring it great blessings and enrich its life, but which it could no doubt do without. This is not one of them. If it had not been for the tears of Monica, the Church would have no St. Augustine. The whole world today is an Augustine, waiting for the redemptive tears which will bring upon it the grace of God and restore it to life in Him.

There is a prayer in the missal which begs for the gift of tears: it is a grace we all need for ourselves, and we ought to ask for it. But you who have this work to do in the world, need to ask for it with special urgency. When

Augustine is describing how he tricked his mother and set out secretly for Rome, he speaks of her as with sorrow seeking what with sorrow she had brought forth. Constantly he reverts to the idea of her double motherhood: she brought him forth, he says, both in her flesh, that he might be born into this temporal light, and in her heart, that he might be born into the Light Eternal. As it was through the pains of childbirth that she brought him into the world of time, so it was through the agony of her sorrow for his sins and her fears for his soul that she brought him forth again into the life of eternity. She brought him forth again in her heart. If you are to do the work she did, either for particular human beings or for the world as a whole, you must have a heart like hers.

But this comparison between the birth in the flesh and the birth in the spirit leads us on to think of another — and essential — aspect, of the vocation of tears. You remember the words of our Lord: "A woman, when she is in labor, hath sorrow because her hour is come; but when she hath brought forth the child, she remembereth no more the anguish, for joy that a man is born into the world."[52] And you remember that our Lord uses

[52]John 16:21.

this as an illustration of what He has just said to His disciples about themselves: "You shall be made sorrowful, but your sorrow shall be turned into joy."[53]

The sorrow we have been thinking of so far has to be set beside that joy which is an essential quality of the true Christian, if it is to be seen aright. Compare, in the *Confessions*, Augustine's grief over his mother's death with his earlier grief over his friend. When his friend dies, Augustine is plunged into despair: "I became a great puzzle to myself," he writes, "and I asked my soul why it was so sad and why so disquieted within me; and it knew not what to answer. And if I said, 'Trust thou in God,' it rightly did not obey; for that dearest one whom it had lost was both truer and better than that phantasm in which it was bidden to trust."[54] But when his mother dies, his sorrow is not unrelieved bitterness, for in the meantime, he has found God in his heart; and so, "it was a comfort to me," he says to God, "to weep in Thy sight, concerning her and for myself, concerning myself and for her."[55] And he is not compelled,

[53]John 16:20.
[54]*Confessions*, Bk. 4, ch. 4.
[55]Ibid., Bk. 9, ch. 12.

as he was in the former case, to try to forget the sorrow by seeking for new joys; the sorrow itself is gradually turned into joy.

⚭

The fruit of suffering is joy

There is indeed in the human heart a strange power of housing joy and sorrow together, and you find it very clearly in the saints, who seem most gay and untroubled when they are suffering most. You find it in one of those small revealing touches with which Augustine paints for us his mother's personality, when he says that to the women who complained to her of the violent treatment they suffered at the hands of their husbands, she gave grave advice, but as if in jest.

"Your sorrow shall be turned into joy." We should compare this saying of our Lord with another one: "And when you fast, be not as the hypocrites, sad."[56] You have to *believe*, first of all, that out of all the evil, good will eventually come. Secondly, you have to believe that your tears, if they are shed in God's sight, will themselves help to bring forth the good from the evil. Thirdly,

[56] Matt. 6:16.

therefore, you have to be glad even in your sorrow, because your sorrow is such that God will incline His ear to it and turn it into joy — by bringing joy and rest to those for whom you sorrow.

And as joy is an essential part of the Christian life, so it is in particular an essential part of the vocation of tears, not only because in the sorrow there is always the joy of hope, but because if the sorrow turns into gloom, it ceases to be redemptive. You cannot offer a sacrifice of praise with sullen lips; if you are going to offer God your tears and penances for the saving of souls, you must first of all have the faith and hope and love whose joy is never extinguished.

"Blessed is he who loves Thee, and his friend in Thee, and his enemy for Thee," wrote Augustine in prayer to God, "for he alone loses no one dear to him, to whom all are dear in the One who can never be lost."[57] Such a person is blessed, because he will never despair, but will make his sorrow a sacrifice of praise. And he is blessed also because his sorrows will fulfill the vocation of tears, in the second sense we considered earlier: they will themselves bring comfort and

[57]*Confessions*, Bk. 4, ch. 9.

light to other hearts because of the joy that goes with them.

If Monica had perpetually nagged her son, if she had been always weeping and wailing in his presence, she would have driven him not to God, but to desperation. His mother kept the words in her heart. The tears must be shed in secret, to God; to the world you must show laughter and joy.

✣

The vocation of tears can be fulfilled daily

Let us return for a moment to family life, and see these ideas there, in their most obvious setting. What we have to keep reminding ourselves of is this: the vocation of tears is not a high-flown romantic fantasy, but part of the ordinary living of an ordinary, humdrum life. You find saints who suffer incredible things for the saving of the world, yes; but these are the exceptions. What you must try to imitate is not their extraordinary ways of expiating for the world's sins, but the extraordinary love and joy and single-mindedness with which they bear their crosses.

You can perfectly well carry out this vocation to the full by doing nothing more elaborate and alarming than what is provided by the ordinary drudgery of kitchen and nursery. You can also carry it out by accepting without gloom and despondency the inevitable evolution of married life from the romantic glamour of the first days to the less exciting but more important work of building the family in oneness of mind which follows. If you try to cling to the glamour at all costs, and therefore run away from the duties of motherhood and the work of making a home, you miss the realities of life; the glamour will fade despite your efforts, and then you will find you have nothing with which to replace it.

If, on the other hand, you accept the fact that the making of a family together implies and effects a change from the early glamour to the later, more pedestrian, but deeper, unity of mind and heart, then you will not only experience the realities of life, but will also fulfill, without fuss but with lasting effect, this vocation we have been considering. Although you will have your full share of disappointment and discomfort and hard work and self-discipline, they will stand you and your family in good stead in the day of need, if you live them always in the sight of God, and for the love of God, and turn them — and your family through them — into the joy and happiness that are the fruits of living with God.

The same is true in substance of work in the world. It is possible that God wants of you some extraordinary self-dedication; it is far more probable that He wants you only to turn the ordinary everyday troubles and crosses of life into joy. Every form of work has its hardships, strains, and boredoms; every friendship has its problems and its crosses; every day has its incidental vexations. Physical pain, mental worry, the sorrows of the heart: if you take them all as coming from God's hands and force yourself to be merry in spite of them, so that the world knows you for the depth of your understanding and sympathy, but also for the constancy of your gaiety, you will be fulfilling your vocation. And quite apart from the debt it owes you indirectly, for the graces you have earned for it, the world will be your debtor immediately and directly, because, like Monica, you will bring it peace.

⚭

Seek St. Monica's intercession
Pray to Monica to obtain for you her own gift of tears, so that like her you may help to make up what is wanting in the sufferings of Christ, in your flesh, for the Church. Pray to Monica to obtain for you the sense of

sin and the will to expiate, for only if we have been planted together in the likeness of the death of Christ shall we be also in the likeness of His Resurrection.

Pray to her that you may learn to say, and help the world to say, "*De profundis*," and to say it with sorrow and yet with hope and joy because of the Man who is born into the world, and in whom all other men may be born again. So you will do glory to God and good to men, for it is only when we have learned to say, "*De profundis*" from our hearts that we can merit — and help the world to merit — the grace to say, "Glory to God in the highest,"[58] and to have what follows from it: peace on earth.

[58]Luke 2:14.

❦

Lead souls to God through love

She shall crush thy head, and
thou shalt lie in wait for her heel.

Genesis 3:15

⚜

To study the life of our Lady or St. Monica is to gain an impression of an influence silent, secret, self-effacing, patient; working in the background. But we shall miss its meaning if we think of it as something passive, or as limited to the task of supporting and sustaining, comforting and encouraging, expiating. It is active and creative; it not only sustains activity, but calls it forth.

That is indeed the most obvious fact about woman throughout the course of history: it is her fate to bring out either what is best or what is worst in men. They will perform Herculean feats of bravery to win her, or they will cheat and lie and do crimes of violence; they will fight among themselves for her; for her sake they will become wise and strong and gentle, or they will sink into a servility and a degradation which, in the end, empty them of their manhood.

Heart of Compassion

One of the old Greek thinkers spoke of God as being the cause of all things insofar as He is that which all things desire and aspire to and are moved to reach out to by their own growth and fulfillment. In something of the same way, it is the destiny of woman to lead man to action through the leadership of love. Our Lord said, "When I shall be lifted up, I shall draw all things to me."[59] Whether her summons shall lead men to Heaven or to Hell depends upon the extent to which woman possesses within her, like St. Catherine, the heart of Christ. We can see the two possible alternatives very clearly if we look at the contrasting figures of Eve in the story of Genesis and Beatrice in the *Divine Comedy* of Dante.[60]

Eve sinned in defiance of her feminine wisdom
You remember how the story of the Fall of man begins. The Serpent was more subtle than any of the beasts of the earth which the Lord God had made. The Devil is a clever debater, skilled in the art of making argument

[59]John 12:32.
[60]Dante Alighieri (1265-1321), Italian poet and philosopher. Beatrice is Dante's guide through Paradise in his *Divine Comedy*.

appear to do service to truth when it is actually masking falsehood; it should have been the prerogative of Eve to answer his parade of reason with her own feminine wisdom. "Why hath God commanded you, that you should not eat of every tree of Paradise?" he asks her, and she replies that it is not every tree: it is only one tree that they are forbidden to eat of, or indeed touch, lest they die.[61] You notice the childlike exaggeration: "We are not even allowed to touch it," she tells him, so deeply had the importance of the command of God impressed her.

But she was not childlike enough. The symbolism is not of some obvious crime that is forbidden them, but of something in itself indifferent, because it is of the essence of their nature as creatures to acknowledge the power and the right of God to command — to accept the idea that, as Julian of Norwich[62] tells us, God has not only the knowledge which He makes known to us, but His secret knowledge also, which none can seek to know. She should have preserved the humility before God which is proper to her wisdom; but the fruit was fair to the eyes and delightful to behold: "Your eyes shall

---

[61]Gen. 3:1-3.
[62]Julian of Norwich (c. 1342-1413), English mystic.

be opened, and you shall be as gods,"[63] the Serpent told her — as gods: autonomous, deciding for themselves what shall be good and what shall be evil. Her belief in the divine threat was shaken, and her trust in the divine goodness with it. And she took the fruit and ate it, and gave to her husband, who ate it.[64]

She had exercised her influence, but because it was in defiance of her feminine wisdom, it was baleful. And their eyes *were* opened, the story goes on, with that irony which in the Old Testament, as in the New, seems so often to cloak the sorrow and the compassion of God. They perceived themselves to be naked — and indeed they were: conscious of their lost integrity, bereft, cut off from God. And they sewed together fig leaves and made themselves aprons[65] — no longer a king and queen, but like naughty children ashamed of themselves.

"And as the day wore on, they heard the Lord God walking in Paradise, and they hid themselves, so that God called to Adam and said to him, 'Where art thou?'"[66] Hitherto they had walked with Him in the evenings;

[63]Gen. 3:5.
[64]Gen. 3:6.
[65]Gen. 3:7.
[66]Cf. Gen. 3:8-9.

they had been contemplatives, sharing in His life. Now they would be able to no longer; they would have to grope for Him, as we have to grope for Him now.

And then Adam tries to put the blame on the woman whom God had given him, and so to put it yet further back, on God Himself. And Eve, in her turn, says that the Serpent deceived her — as indeed he had deceived her with his forensic guile, when she should have been listening to the voice of her own God-given wisdom.

And then, finally, there comes the judgment, the sorrows that will be multiplied for the woman; but there comes also the promise and the hope: "I will put enmities between thee and the woman," God says to the Serpent, "and between thy seed and her seed. She shall crush thy head, and thou shalt lie in wait for her heel."[67]

Woman should lead others to God through love
We have been thinking of Monica as the woman who brought forth her son, first in the flesh, into the light of this material world, and then in her heart, into the Light Eternal; and we have been thinking of the way in

[67]Gen. 3:15.

which all women are meant to share in the work of bringing back souls to God, to rebirth in the Light Eternal, through their prayers and their tears. The Genesis story takes us a step further. The mission of woman is not merely a passive, expiatory one; it is the active mission of the leadership of love.

The words of God to the Serpent carry in them the promise of the Word made flesh, and as Mary is to bring forth the Son who shall crush the Serpent's head,[68] so it is the destiny of all who share in her vocation of spiritual motherhood to bring forth in their hearts those who will share in her Son's battle against evil. It is the destiny of woman to form man, by her active leadership, into the likeness of Christ; to help him to return to the source of life and knowledge and power: in other words, to reverse the primal sin, to reject the creature's attempt to be as a god, and to recognize the limitations of human reason and the true emancipation of the human will which is obedience to God. It is her destiny to show man, by being herself God's handmaid, how to

---

[68]It makes little difference whether we read, with the Vulgate, "*She* shall crush thy head," or with other manuscripts, "*It*," the seed which is Christ, "shall crush thy head."

rise to the fullness of his stature; how to accept the destiny of shared divinity which is offered him, by humbly accepting the essential powerlessness of the humanity which is his natural state.

How is she to do all this? By the twofold office of love: by teaching, and by empowering, encouraging, and drawing onward to life. This twofold office we shall see fulfilled in the figure of Beatrice. We shall see it there in its clearest and most cogent form; but we must not narrow down to a particular type of relationship what is of itself a universal vocation. The story of Dante and Beatrice corresponds and contrasts with the story of Adam and Eve, the world's first lovers, and applies most immediately to other lovers. But it has its general application, and we shall come to it later on. Let us first recall the story itself.

⚜

Love must sometimes be severe

Beatrice, like Eve, is in the earthly Paradise when we first meet her, and when Dante first meets her again, in the *Divine Comedy*. And let us notice the stages of their meeting, for first it is not by sight that he realizes her presence; rather, by a hidden influence which proceeds from her, he becomes conscious of the mighty power of his early love. And then, when she bids him look at her — "Look well, I am, I am indeed Beatrice"[69] — he is filled with overwhelming shame.

She seems to him as commanding as a mother appears to her son, for there is a bitterness in the flavor of severe pity. As commanding as a mother: we misunderstand love completely and degrade it if we confuse it with a soft sentimentality. Love is what seeks the good of the one loved, and sometimes that must imply severity. Beatrice in fact rebukes him roundly — she makes him cry. She rebukes him for having deserted her.

For a time, she had sustained him by her countenance; by displaying her youthful eyes to him she led him with her in the right way. But when she was twenty-five, she died, and he, forsaking her memory, had given his heart to another. We do not know who this other girl was; as a symbol, she has been taken by commentators to mean philosophy as opposed to theology. We might say rather that she symbolizes reason as spoiled and diminished by its attempt to be autonomous, as opposed to the wisdom which is the gift of God; for as a

---

[69]*Divine Comedy*, "Purgatory," canto 30, line 73.

symbol, it is from the primal sin that she seeks to recall us. And she goes on to say how all her efforts to save him were of no avail, and there was only one thing left to do: to show him the lost people.

Either the pride of reason independent of God must be allowed to go on until it destroys all that it has built, so that then the soul may realize where its true greatness lies; or else it must be shown how it *will* in fact inevitably destroy itself, by being shown the lost people, the people who have come to the tragic end of the process and are fixed, by their own will, in destruction. Then, if the journey through the *Inferno* has had its effect, if the exploration of the deep underworld and what it reveals of sunken humanity has opened the soul once again to the sense of depth and of the need of redemption, so that it can cry for the mercy of God and the grace of rebirth, then it is possible, and it is time, for Beatrice to begin the second part of her mission; to reveal to him something of the life and the nature of God.

⁜

Woman must lead man to God
And how is this to be accomplished? Remember in the *Divine Comedy* the song sung by the three ladies as

they come forward dancing: "Turn, Beatrice, turn your eyes to your faithful one, who has journeyed so far to have sight of you."[70] And they beg her to unveil her face, and reveal her smile to Dante. A thousand longings, hotter than flame, fix his eyes upon her radiant eyes, but then upon the Gryphon, the figure who represents Christ; and in the eyes of Beatrice, like the sun reflected in a glass, it is the Gryphon that he sees. And when, at the behest of the three ladies, she reveals her holy smile, and he is so rapt in gazing that his other senses are as though in abeyance, still she will not let him deny her true nature and his by idolatry: it is to the Gryphon that she is to lead him.

A thousand longings fixed his eyes upon her radiant eyes, but they were steadfastly fixed upon the Gryphon. That is the central point, the essence of the leadership of love. The woman is not to be merely that *through* which God is revealed: she is also to be that *in* which God is revealed. To fulfill her office, she must have the gift of kindling and keeping his love, but she must herself be filled with the sight of God — not to forget man, but to lead him with her.

[70]*Divine Comedy*, "Purgatory," canto 31, lines 133-135.

So she reverses the thing that Eve had done; she reverses the primal sin, and in doing so, she reverses the effect of it upon man. It is not without good reason that the poet, as he goes on to describe the procession through the forest, reminds us that it was uninhabited because of the sin of her who had trusted the Serpent. And later they come to the tree whose boughs are bare of leaf and flower, the tree of knowledge of good and evil, and they praise the Gryphon because He has not plucked anything from it. Then finally the tree itself is renewed as the Gryphon ties to it a chariot-pole, which represents the Cross — the wood on which the rebellion of Adam was wiped out by the perfect self-dedication of man, in the person of the Son, to God.

⚬

The ultimate object of love is God

The first office of love in its leadership is to teach. But its essential method of teaching is not to expound, to reason, or to demonstrate to the mind; it is to reveal to the heart of the lover the truth as incarnate in the object loved. If you see the truth coldly and objectively stated, it may fail to compel you; if you see it shining in the eyes you love, it will become, like them, a part of yourself. It is the prerogative of love that it can cause the truth to become in this way identified with what is loved, so that the truth itself is seen in a new way. It becomes, as theologians say, "connatural": possessed, realized as part of the felt oneness of the two who love — no longer the material of a cold intellectual judgment, but something which immediately draws the heart.

St. Paul speaks of the difficulty of loving the God whom we cannot see, as compared with the created beauty which we can see:[71] it is the privilege and the responsibility of Beatrice to reveal the invisible to man, so ready to become immersed in the visible and the material. That is why she is given the privilege of her wisdom and her power. And it is not only a privilege, but a hard responsibility, because it is so easy on earth to misuse the power. It is so easy for the woman to fail to keep her eyes fixed steadfastly on the Gryphon, so that when the man gazes at them, he sees not God, but only her. Eve had the power, and she used it wrongly because she herself was led astray after a supposed independence of judgment and will which was in direct contradiction to her nature.

[71]Cf. Rom. 1:20-23.

Beatrice had the power, but she used it to redeem and lead back to God, because she herself loved God above all things, and all things in God. So, as the hand-maid of the Mediator, she mediates in her turn: she draws man to know and love her so that she may then lead him beyond herself to that Beauty of which she and all things else are but a pale and partial reflection. She leads him to the Cross, and when he in his turn goes back to the world to work in it for the fulfilling of the redemptive purposes of Christ, she is in his work and the glory of it, for it is she who has made it possible by bringing him forth in her heart into the Eternal Light.

Woman should direct man to the Eternal Light
But love not only teaches: it spurs to action; it leads. Beatrice does more than cause Dante to gaze on Christ. "Fix your eyes now," she says, "upon the chariot; and what you see, be sure you write it when you return to earth."[72] It is not a command which he will find diffi-cult or distasteful to carry out; there could hardly be a

---

[72]*Divine Comedy*, "Purgatory," canto 32, lines 101-103.

greater incentive to write than to be told to write by love.

Love, like wisdom, reaches from end to end mightily, but disposes all things sweetly.[73] Fear or force can produce action by compulsion, forcing on, as it were, from behind, but love produces action by a free and glad impulsion, drawing onward from in front. It is because Dante is led by his love to understand something of infinite Love, and so to be in a state of love toward all men, that he is impelled in all his actions to spread through the world the spirit of that Love — the spirit of Christ the Savior. As long as the influence remains with him, all his actions are colored and informed by the charity which possesses him, and so they become healing and saving for the souls of men.

That is what love's leadership can do in its twofold office. By leading her beloved to God as revealed in herself, she gives him the sense of his ultimate destiny and direction. She gives him a sense of men's brotherhood in God. She gives him a glimpse of the immensities of the destiny offered him, the heights he is to scale, the Heaven which awaits him. She gives him, in his own

[73]Wisd. 8:1.

shame, a sense of his own blindness and stupidity, and therefore prepares him for the grace of humility and patience and the power to learn. In other words, she gives him the sense of the length and breadth and height and depth, and when he has once been given that, he can begin to live, to accept and exult in the grace and the stature of the sons of God.

So Beatrice fulfills the destiny for which she was given her radiant eyes: her beloved sees her gazing like an eagle at the Sun, and is therefore impelled to do the same. And when, unable any longer to endure the brilliant light, he withdraws his eyes from it, it is only to fix them upon her, and so to find himself changed by looking. Higher and higher he climbs, led onward by her eyes and her smile, until at last he can gaze even on the blinding glory of the "light inaccessible"[74] of the Godhead.

And so his journey ends, in "the Eternal Light that alone abides within itself,"[75] that alone knows itself, and, known and knowing, loves and smiles. And her journey, her mission, is ended too. "She who has thus imparadised

[74] 1 Tim. 6:16.
[75] *Divine Comedy*, "Paradise," canto 33, lines 124-125.

his spirit"[76] has brought him forth in her heart into the Light Eternal, and his love for her is complete and full at last because at last it is caught up into the still, wordless wonder and joy of the "the Love which moves the sun and the other stars."[77]

Love is a lifework

The story of Dante and Beatrice has its first and most obvious application in the everyday married life of men and women. You do not rob the leadership of love of its substance or its importance by taking away something of the poetry and glamour with which the *Divine Comedy* presents it. On the contrary, you misunderstand it completely if you suppose that its validity is confined to the glamorous honeymoon stage of married life, just as you misunderstand love completely if you suppose that it passes with the passing of the first romantic idyll. It is then that it should be just beginning.

And as the real substance of love begins only as the real and deep unity of mind and heart begins, so it may

[76]Ibid., canto 28, line 1.
[77]Ibid., line 145.

be with love's leadership. For it is a lifework, and as it never ceases to be necessary, so it need never cease to exercise its power, however much the quality of the power itself may change. And the effect of the power may in fact become greater, rather than less, as life goes on and becomes more pedestrian; for passion can make a man a willing slave, but a blind one, so that he obeys because he loves, but without conviction; without seeing and loving the truth in the eyes he loves, and obeying that.

As the wife becomes the mother, and gives herself to the second stage of her vocation, she is right, of course, in preserving the substance of the first stage, and in expecting of the man that he will preserve it too, that he will continue to regard her, as before, as a lover. But the fact that he sees in her now, in addition, the commanding stature, not of a goddess remote upon her pedestal, but — as Dante saw Beatrice — of a mother, should mean that what he learns from her will be far more clearly seen in itself and therefore far less ephemeral, far less entangled with the self-regardingness of his passion, and therefore far more purely divine.

What must she do? She must, first of all, be a contemplative; she must learn how to look upon the Sun. Then she must learn the vocation of tears. She must learn how to sympathize, to co-suffer; she must learn how to have compassion and how to comfort and sustain. But she must learn also to be strong enough to have, like Beatrice, the kind of compassion in which there is also a taste of severity; resisting the temptation to do his will when it is stupid or sinful even though he may think her refusal a denial of love.

And as her prayer and her pain and her joys and her labors teach her the wisdom which is divine, so that in her eyes there begins to shine the reflection of the eternal light, so she will teach him to turn to her, not as to a rival of God or of the work which God would have him do, but as the one who will empower him for his work and help him to do it wisely and humbly in the sight of God. And she will labor, as Monica did in her life with Patricius, not in impatient distress at the difficulties and failures of every day, but with her eyes on the distant horizon; on the end of the journey when at last she will have imparadised his heart.

❧

The world needs holy women
Let us turn to the wider application of these themes. The condition of the world is determined by the interplay

of the spiritual influences which at any given time characterize it and, in the last resort, by the one which preponderates. A society in which the vast majority hold that science is all — and suit their actions and ambitions to their belief — will be a world both governed and circumscribed by scientific standards. A society in which the vast majority believe in the *mystique de la force*, the idea that might is in itself something divine, will be a world in which savagery is the accepted weapon of achievement and political self-glorification the only aim.

We have known a world determined very largely by the ambitions of scientific humanism on the one hand, and the assumption of individualism on the other. The aim is an ever-increasing measure of comfort, efficiency, and speed; the assumption, that each man must fend for himself and look to his own advancement.

And recently we have witnessed, in some parts of our world, a movement of reaction to these ways of thought; but it is a reaction, alas, whereby these devils have only been replaced by others worse than themselves.[78] Belief in scientific reason has given way to a

[78]Matt. 12:45; Luke 11:26.

woolly pseudo-mysticism, which at best is the easy prey of delusions and at worst is no more than a subrational and fanatic devotion to a personification of the might of the herd.

Individualism has been replaced by a sense of unity; but a unity in which the individual is submerged and the personality destroyed. It is not thus that the world can be saved. The essential need of the West, even judging by the narrowest human and natural standards, is an evolution of thought which will preserve the hard-won values of individual personality while at the same time restoring the sense of community, so that there may emerge a society that is neither a simple aggregate of individuals nor a blind and unselfconscious herd, but a family.

But to say this is to say that the essential need of the West is the restoration of those qualities of the vocation of woman which we have been considering. And we who believe that the first and greatest need of every society is the need for God, and that its ultimate aim is the building of a life which can be a preparation for God, can see how immense and how urgent the same need is. For without these qualities in our life, we miss the one thing necessary, and all other achievements are but straw. "Unless God build the house, they labor in vain that build it."[79]

Our actions, no matter how trivial, influence others
The same essential responsibility rests upon you, the same opportunity is open to you, whatever your life and your work in the world. You cannot live in the world at all without influencing it to some extent, for better or for worse. Your immediate influence may be confined to a small group with whom you share your work or your leisure hours, and you may be one of those quiet and retiring people who outwardly seem to exercise no influence on others at all. But you influence others by what you are much more than by what you do or say, and although they may be few, they influence others in their turn.

If you are fulfilling your vocation within yourself, you need not be anxious about its effect in the world. God may call you to important active work, or he may want you to live in retirement and solitude; in either case, your essential task remains the same: to make sure

[79]Ps. 126:1 (RSV = Ps. 127:1).

you are becoming the sort of person He would have you be. You have to become a contemplative, and learn to look upon the Sun. You have to learn, through prayer and detachment and the slow growth of wisdom, to love the world aright — in God — and to acquire the hunger and thirst for justice which will make you want to serve it. You have to fulfill in your heart the vocation of tears, learning to have within you the heart of Christ, and therefore the compassion of Christ.

And then, if you are doing all these things, you need not worry about their utility to the world you have learned to love. For if God does not send you out into the world, you will find that the world will begin to come, little by little, to you. No doubt it will not flock to you in any dramatic way, but some will seek you out in the small unnoticed way in which they have sought out some of the saints — and as you know, when history looks back upon them, it sees in them one of the forces which have shaped the spirit of their age.

They will begin to look to you, if you have learned all these things, not only for understanding and sympathy, but for the wisdom which can inspire and lead. They will look to you as to a mediator, who can show them the things of God in terms of the life of man.

They will begin to see in you, whatever your way of life, something of the commanding stature of motherhood, and something of the beauty of holy living wherewith God has made you beautiful. You will speak to them, even though you are silent, of things of which perhaps they would otherwise have never thought, but which they may come to recognize as the pearl of great price,[80] the search for which makes all other ambitions, by comparison, insignificant. You will reveal to them — and through them, to the world — something of the length and breadth and height and depth; and so you will have your share in the redemptive work of Christ. You will have your share in restoring to the world the deep wisdom it has lost, the unity toward which it ineffectually strives, and, finally, the peace for which it longs.

If there are enough in the world to accept the vocation of woman, and really to *fulfill* it, it is they who will save from ruin and turn to good the social ambitions, the political plannings, and the reasoned search for a reasonable world order, which are the work of man. That work is, of course, necessary for the world, just as the work of the husband is necessary to the family.

[80]Matt. 13:46.

115

❧

Man and woman together can transform the world
We have been concerned in these meditations only with the vocation of woman; and perhaps sometimes it has appeared as though the man had little of his own to contribute to the life of the family and the world. That would be an absurd distortion of the truth. A man may in fact contribute nothing but folly; but then so may a woman. We are concerned here with what ought to be. The man and the woman each have an essential contribution to make, and each is an essentially different contribution. The man has to teach in his turn; he has to lead to God; he has to bear sorrows and responsibilities. But all these things he must do in a different way, the way of practical reason and judgment, of reasoned initiative; the way of the wisdom of a masculine mind which even in an Augustine or a John of the Cross[81] is never quite the same as the wisdom that is born in a woman's heart.

The safety and salvation of the world depend on the combined work of man and woman alike; if either fails,

---

[81]St. John of the Cross (1542-1591), mystical Doctor and joint founder of the Discalced Carmelites.

the world must fail. But it remains true that we in this age have been living under a system in which the masculine mind predominates, and we desperately need the fullness of the vocation of woman.

The saints guide us in our mission of love

She shall crush the head of the Serpent. Pray to Mary and to the other saints who have carried out so completely and so gloriously the work of woman. Pray to them first to obtain for you their humility and their readiness to be taught by God, that so you may come to share in their wisdom and patience and strength and power. Learn to say with Mary, "Behold the handmaid of the Lord," and then you will also have a part in the saving of the generations that are with you and the generations that are yet to come. You will be able to say with something of her exaltation and her humility something resembling her magnificat, for He that is mighty will have done great things in you and through you — and in you and through you, His name will be magnified.

And however apparently unromantic your life, you will be able to say with Beatrice, "Look well at me, for I am the one of whom the song was sung by those around the chariot: Blessed who cometh in the name of the Lord."[82] And the generations of man will call you blessed because in you the mission of Beatrice will have been again fulfilled. The wisdom of your eyes and the compassion and gaiety of your smile will have led them to the splendors of the light inaccessible — your eyes, because within them, men will have learned to look upon the image of the Gryphon, and your smile, because in it men will have learned to realize that it is the smile of Christ.

[82]Cf. *Divine Comedy*, "Purgatory," canto 30, line 73; canto 32, lines 84-87.

✂

Biographical note

Gerald Vann, O.P.
(1906-1963)

❧

Born in England in 1906, Gerald Vann entered the Dominican Order in 1923 and, after completing his theological studies in Rome, was ordained a priest in 1929. On returning to England, he studied modern philosophy at Oxford and was then sent to Blackfriars School in Northhamptonshire to teach and later to serve as headmaster of the school and superior of the community there. Tireless in his efforts to bolster the foundations of peace, he organized the international Union of Prayer for Peace during his tenure at Blackfriars.

Fr. Vann devoted his later years to writing, lecturing, and giving retreats in England and in the United States, including giving lectures at The Catholic University of America in Washington, DC.

He wrote numerous articles and books, including a biography of St. Thomas Aquinas, who influenced him greatly. Fr. Vann's writings combine the philosophy and theology of St. Thomas with the humanism emphasized in the 1920s and 1930s. His works reflect his keen understanding of man's relationship to God, his deep sensitivity to human values, and his compassionate understanding of man's problems and needs. Particularly relevant in today's divided world is his appeal for unity, charity, and brotherhood. His elucidating words reveal what it means today to fulfill the two greatest commandments: to love God and to love one's neighbor.

❦

Sophia Institute Press®

Sophia Institute is a nonprofit institution that seeks to restore man's knowledge of eternal truth, including man's knowledge of his own nature, his relation to other persons, and his relation to God.

Sophia Institute Press® serves this end in numerous ways. It publishes translations of foreign works to make them accessible for the first time to English-speaking readers. It brings back into print books that have been long out of print. And it publishes important new books that fulfill the ideals of Sophia Institute. These books afford readers a rich source of the enduring wisdom of mankind.

Sophia Institute Press® makes these high-quality books available to the general public by using advanced technology and by soliciting donations to subsidize its general publishing costs.

Your generosity can help Sophia Institute Press® to provide the public with editions of works containing the enduring wisdom of the ages. Please send your tax-deductible contribution to the address below.

The members of the Editorial Board of Sophia Institute Press® welcome questions, comments, and suggestions from all our readers.

For your free catalog, call:
Toll-free: 1-800-888-9344

or write:
Sophia Institute Press®
Box 5284
Manchester, NH 03108

or visit our website at:
http://www.sophiainstitute.com

Sophia Institute is a tax-exempt institution
as defined by the Internal Revenue Code,
Section 501(c)(3). Tax I.D. 22-2548708